JUL 1 1 2001

Dr. Martin Luther King, Jr.

by
David A. Adler

illustrated by
Colin Bootman

Holiday House / New York

For Nathan and Beth,
Rachel, Michal, Rena, and Aliza
D. A. A.

For Meisha Bootman,
my loving sister, and her sons,
Andre and Wade
C. B.

Library of Congress Cataloging-in-Publication Data
Adler, David A.
Dr. Martin Luther King, Jr. / David A. Adler; illustrated by Colin Bootman.—1st ed.
p.   cm.
Summary: Tells the story of Dr. Martin Luther King, Jr., his life,
accomplishments in the civil rights movement, and his impact on American history.
ISBN 0-8234-1572-4
1. King, Martin Luther, Jr., 1929–1968—Juvenile literature.
2. Afro-Americans—Biography—Juvenile literature. 3. Civil rights workers—
United States—Biography—Juvenile literature. 4. Baptists—United States—
Clergy—Biography—Juvenile literature. 5. Afro-Americans—Civil rights—
History—20th century—Juvenile literature. [1. King, Martin Luther, Jr., 1929–1968.
2. Civil rights workers. 3. Clergy. 4. Civil rights movements—History.
5. Afro-Americans—Biography.]
I. Bootman, Colin, ill. II. Title.

E185.97.K5 A627 2001
323′.092—dc21
[B]   00-024314

Contents

1. Young Martin Luther King, Jr.

Martin Luther King, Jr.,
was born in 1929,
in Atlanta, Georgia.
His father was a minister.
His mother was a teacher.
Martin learned early
that because he was
African American,
because he was black,
many places were
closed to him.

In Atlanta and other places
there were lots
of WHITES ONLY signs.
Many hotels, restaurants,
railroad cars, parks, pools,
and schools
were closed
to African Americans.
In many cities,
blacks could ride only
in the back of buses.
They could only
sit in the balcony
of movie theaters.
They could only enter
through the back door
of white people's homes.

When Martin was six years old,
he was told that two of his friends
could not play with him anymore.
This was because he was black
and they were white.

Martin went home and cried.
He did not understand.
Why did the color of his skin
matter to some people?

Martin's mother and grandmother
told him about hate and prejudice.
They also told him
he was as good as anyone.

Martin said later
they taught him
"somebodiness."

11

2. Martin's Father

Martin's father was
a proud man. He hated the way
African Americans were treated.

"The law may force me
   to ride in the back," he told his son,
"but my mind is always up front."

Martin went with his father once
to buy shoes.
The clerk told them to wait
in the back of the store.
Martin's father said no.
He would buy shoes
in the front of the store
or not at all.
Then he took Martin's hand.
They walked out of the store.

Each Sunday, Martin heard
his father speak in church.
His father held people's attention
with the power of his words
and the power of his ideas.
Martin told his mother,
"I'm going to get me some big words."

Martin read and studied.

He was a good student.

By the time he was fifteen,
he was already in college.

By the time he was eighteen,
he was a minister.

After college, Martin went
to Boston
to study some more.
There he met Coretta Scott.
They went together to movies
and concerts.
They met for lunches
and dinners.
They talked and talked.
They fell in love.

Martin Luther King, Jr., and
Coretta Scott married in June 1953.
In 1954 Martin Luther King, Jr., took
a job as a minister in Montgomery,
Alabama. He completed his studies
the next year. He was then Dr. King.

3. The Montgomery Bus Boycott

On Thursday, December 1, 1955,
in Montgomery, Alabama,
a bus driver told four African Americans
to get up. He told them
to give up their seats to white riders.

Three of the
African Americans
got up.
One did not.
Rosa Parks stayed in her seat.
She was arrested.
On Monday, December 5,
a judge said she broke the law.

Dr. King led a protest against
this unfair law.
African Americans in Montgomery
stopped riding public buses.
Dr. King made speeches.

He led the Montgomery bus boycott.

People were angry.

They were ready to fight.

Dr. King said,

"We must meet hate with love."

For more than a year,
African Americans
in Montgomery
stayed off public buses.
Then the United States
Supreme Court
ruled it was against the law
to force black people
to give their seats
to whites.
It was against the law
to keep blacks
in the back of the bus.

No. 342. GAYLE ET AL., MEMBERS OF THE BOARD OF COMMISSIONERS OF MONTGOMERY, ALABAMA, ET AL. v. BROWDER ET AL.; and

No. 343. OWEN ET AL., MEMBERS OF THE ALABAMA PUBLIC SERVICE COMMISSION, ET AL. v. BROWDER ET AL.

SUPREME COURT OF THE UNITED STATES

352 U.S. 903; 77 S. Ct. 145; 1956 U.S. LEXIS 199; 1 L. Ed. 2d 114

Nov. 13, 1956.

PRIOR HISTORY:
[*1]
Appeals from the United States District Court for the Middle District of Alabama. Reported below: 142 F. Supp. 707.

COUNSEL:
Walter J. Knabe for appellants in No. 342. John Patterson, Attorney General of Alabama, and William N. McQueen and Gordon Madison, Assistant Attorneys General, for appellants in No. 343. Robert L. Carter and Thurgood Marshall for appellees in No. 343.

OPINION:
Per Curiam: the motion to affirm is granted and the judgment is affirmed. Brown v. Board of Education, 347 U.S. 483; Mayor and City Council of Baltimore v. Dawson, 350 U.S. 877; Holmes v. Atlanta, 350 U.S. 879.

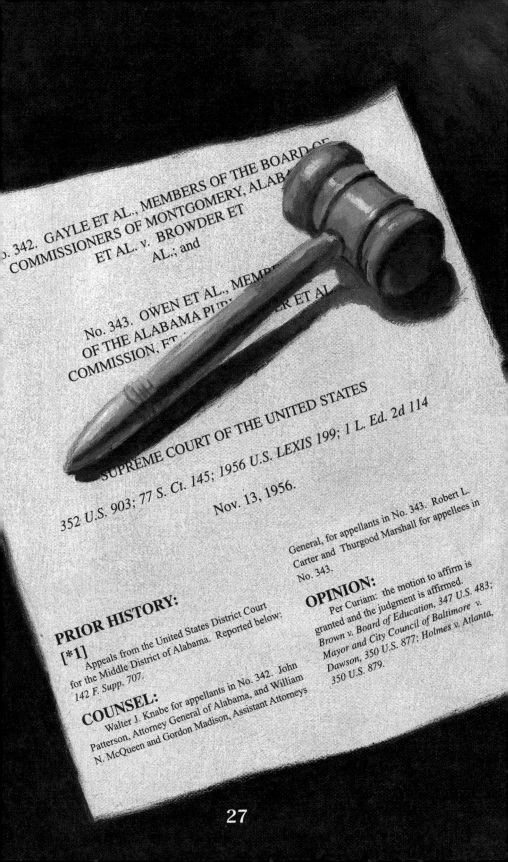

The boycott ended on December 21, 1956.
That day, in Montgomery, Alabama,
Dr. King and Rosa Parks rode
on a public bus. They sat in front.

4. A Powerful Man of Peace

Dr. King was a leader
in the fight for the civil rights
of all people in the United States.

There were "sit-ins".
Black people sat
at whites-only
lunch counters.
They asked to be served.
There were
"freedom rides."

Black and white
freedom riders
rode together on buses.
They sat together
in whites-only waiting rooms.
They used whites-only rest rooms.

There were hundreds
of boycotts and marches
for freedom.

The biggest march of all
was in August 1963.
It was the March on Washington.
Dr. King spoke from the steps
of the Lincoln Memorial.

"I have a dream," he said,
that one day, in our nation,
people "will not be judged
by the color of their skin
but by the content of their character."

Dr. King led the fight for civil rights.

He met with lawmakers and presidents.

He led a peaceful fight.

"If pushed," Dr. King said,

"do not push back.

If struck, do not strike back."

He taught his followers
to fight hate with love.
He was a powerful man of peace.
For his good work,
Dr. King won
the Nobel Peace Prize in 1964.
But surely his greatest prizes

were laws that were passed.
The Civil Rights Act of 1964
and the Voting Rights Act of 1965
protect the rights of people
of all races and religions.

5. Free at Last

In April 1968 Dr. King went
to Memphis, Tennessee.
He planned to march there.
He wanted black and white
garbage workers
to get the same pay
for the same work.

The night before the march,
he stood outside his motel room.
Hidden in a bathroom
across from Dr. King
was James Earl Ray.
Ray aimed his rifle.
He shot and killed Dr. King.

Dr. King had said he dreamed
of a world free of hate, prejudice,
and violence.
The marker on his grave reads,
"I'm free at last."
Dr. King left behind
a wife and four children.
He left behind millions of tearful
black and white Americans,
people who loved and
respected him.

The third Monday in January
is now a national holiday.
It celebrates the life
of Dr. Martin Luther King, Jr.,
a powerful man of peace.

Important Dates

January 15, 1929

Martin Luther King, Jr.,

is born in Atlanta, Georgia.

February 25, 1948

Martin Luther King, Jr., is ordained

as a minister.

June 18, 1953

Coretta Scott and Martin get married.

1955–1956

Dr. King leads the bus boycott in

Montgomery, Alabama.

August 28, 1963

Dr. King gives his famous "I Have a

Dream" speech in Washington, D.C.

December 10, 1964

Dr. King receives the Nobel Peace Prize.

April 4, 1968

James Earl Ray kills Dr. King

in Memphis, Tennessee.

1986

Martin Luther King, Jr., Day

becomes a national holiday.

Sources

Bishop, Jim. *The Days of Martin Luther King, Jr.* New York: G.P. Putnam & Sons, 1971.

Carson, Clayborne, ed. *The Autobiography of Martin Luther King, Jr.* New York: Warner Books, 1998.

King, Coretta Scott. *My Life with Martin Luther King, Jr.* New York: Holt, Rinehart and Winston, 1969.

Oates, Stephen B. *Let the Trumpet Sound: The Life of Martin Luther King, Jr.* New York: Harper & Row, 1982.